McPoems

McPoems

Billeh Nickerson

*For Lynn,
who inspires me.*

xo

*Billeh
Ni—*

Arsenal Pulp Press
Vancouver

McPOEMS

Copyright © 2009 by Billeh Nickerson

ARSENAL PULP PRESS
Suite 200, 341 Water Street
Vancouver, BC
Canada V6B 1B8
arsenalpulp.com

The publisher gratefully acknowledges the support of the Canada Council for the Arts and the British Columbia Arts Council for its publishing program, and the Government of Canada through the Book Publishing Industry Development Program and the Government of British Columbia through the Book Publishing Tax Credit Program for its publishing activities.

Book design by Shyla Seller, based on a concept by Rebecca Watt

Printed and bound in Canada on FSC-certified paper

Library and Archives Canada Cataloguing in Publication

Nickerson, Billeh, 1972-

   McPoems / Billeh Nickerson.

ISBN 978-1-55152-265-4

   1. Fast food restaurants--Poetry. I. Title.

PS8577.I32M36 2009   C811'.6   C2009-903654-1

Mixed Sources
Product group from well-managed forests,
controlled sources and recycled wood or fiber
www.fsc.org Cert no. SW-COC-000952
© 1996 Forest Stewardship Council
FSC

In memory of Elizabeth "Betty" McEwan

"That's it for breakfast, ladies, what you see is what you get."

Contents

Service

Cleanliness

Value

"The recipe for success must always include quality, service, cleanliness, and value. These are your most important ingredients."
—*Your Restaurant Training Manual*

Quality

No Pickle

A grown man cries in front of you after the cooks in the back put a pickle on his burger for the third time this week. Sure, he said *No pickle*, but you can't help thinking even if you hated pickle and asked for something without it you'd get ticked off but you wouldn't cry—not because of a pickle. That guy's not crying because of his burger, it's something else, something you hope isn't contagious as you scoot past the counter, put your arm around him, offer to refill his coke.

Diet

After working every day for two weeks straight
a co-worker points out you always eat the same thing:
two cheeseburgers, a large fries, and a big cola.
You've never thought about them
as separate items before, have barely considered it
a ritual, nothing more than the right amount of food
to induce comfort and satisfaction.
But when she points out you've eaten
twenty-eight cheeseburgers, fourteen large fries
and a kitchen sink's worth of cola,
you make a mental note
to pack a sandwich for lunch tomorrow,
eat an apple, possibly some celery.

Tricks

Sometimes it's grown men with straws attached to their bicuspids so they look like walruses, or people who place their burgers on top of their heads like models in a comportment class. Sometimes it's singers and dancers and mimes who perform their orders, or teenagers who stick their burgers under their sweaters so it looks like they have breasts—especially after the circular burns form on their chests. Your favourite? The guy who orders five cheeseburgers then juggles them out the door.

Wacky Straws

Two days into a month-long promotion
head office recalls the wacky straws
shaped like mascots
as children were sucking too hard
and starting to hyperventilate.

You can't stop thinking
about one little girl in particular—
her face purple with determination
as her too-thick milkshake
slowly snaked its way around
to her mouth—and a friend

who thought he'd impress a pretty new hire
by showing his wacky-straw prowess
only to suck so hard
that he broke a blood vessel in his eye.

Stigmata

Since the Halloween when the skinny hippy guy who looks like Jesus dressed up as Jesus and spent the entire dinner rush in the restaurant foyer dipping French fries into his palms, you've grown tired of fake stigmata. Draculas, werewolves, zombies, all have used your ketchups, as have stupid teenaged boys with maxi-pads on their foreheads. Once when an old man stumbled into the restaurant with blood all over his face, you didn't believe him at first. Wished he could have been a bit more original.

Alchemy

Even you still marvel
at how quickly
everything transforms.
One moment it's frozen,
the next moment golden.

Nuts

When students from the local high school
start to order their sundaes
as either *male* or *female*—
male hot fudge meaning with nuts
female hot fudge meaning without—
one good-hearted manager misunderstands
and tries to convince your customer
the employee's gender won't change the sundae,
everything tastes the same.

Pancakes

At the quarterly staff meeting, the regional manager talks for twenty minutes about mascot-shaped pancakes. How little kids and little kids at heart love to eat food shaped like real-life objects. He speaks of animal crackers, licorice babies, chocolate bunnies, and you picture yourself as a giant pancake, your uniform covered in maple syrup, hundreds of white plastic forks digging in.

Hot Apple Pie

Burns your tongue so badly
you can't taste anything
three days later
when you order another.

The Unicorn

Infamous for many things, but named after only one, the Unicorn always orders a soft-serve cone, then sticks it to the top of his forehead and walks around the restaurant until it melts and slides away. Sometimes the melting takes a few seconds, but other times you'll see him sitting with rivulets of cream trickling down his face, his proud cone still intact. How can you not watch a man with an ice cream cone on his head? It's true, with him they broke the mould, he's one of a kind.

The Lottery

It starts off with the woman
who you predict—correctly—
will order a garden salad and diet coke
though you also know she'll ask
for two packets of the super fattening dressing.
All that day you know who'll order
fish burgers, chicken nuggets, hamburgers
with or without the cheese.
A co-worker begs you to concentrate
on that week's lottery numbers,
asks you to do it for his newborn daughter,
but no matter how hard you focus,
you can only tell that in a few moments
he'll want a strawberry shake.

The Movie Star

A woman you swear is a movie star
comes up to your register,
orders chicken nuggets
with BBQ sauce,
a medium cola,
then changes her mind,
makes you pour another drink,
this time diet.
Had she been any other customer
you would have been ticked off,
but she's a movie star,
her eyes twinkling,
the restaurant as momentarily glamorous
as your job is not.

Service

Local Attraction

When the tour group of non-English speakers arrives
you find yourself acting out the orders,
flapping your arms for chicken,
mooing for every burger, re-enacting an epic struggle
with a fishing pole whenever someone orders a filet.
For those few minutes you are the centre of the universe,
more important than French fries, more important
than mascots, extra napkins, multiple dipping sauces.
For the first time in your life you understand
what it's like to be a celebrity, a local attraction,
the most photographed thing in the room.

St. Patrick's Day

A customer screams
when you explain you're out of the syrup
that makes the holiday shakes green.
He complains about having to wait
a whole year, that you've single-handedly
ruined his entire family's St. Patrick's Day,
how can he show his face at home
with just an ordinary shake—
St. Patrick's Day isn't about chocolate!
Why not order a vanilla
and get some food colouring
you suggest.
Better yet, why not have your kids
drink them in the dark?

Halloween

A drunk clown demands free French fries
tells you to *hurry the hell up*
and don't forget the ketchup.
Superman complains his burger is cold,
Luke Skywalker asks for more salt.
After her third hot fudge sundae
you realize Wonder Woman's
bulletproof bracelets
can't protect her from everything.

Conundrum

Time to lean, time to clean

vs.

Time to lean, time to dream

Twist Cone

Your co-worker sings
Ebony and Ivory every time
she makes a twist cone.
It's like chocolate and vanilla,
she tells you
repeatedly,
so often you begin to hate pianos
almost as much as twist cones,
the people who order them,
co-workers who sing.

The Walk-in Freezer

One time you got stuck in the walk-in, and though you knew someone would eventually need to restock, you kept wiggling your toes to protect them from frostbite. After an hour, you started to wonder what could keep you warm, whether the cardboard boxes could be broken down into blankets, whether you could make pillows from frozen buns. Eventually they found you curled into the fetal position sucking your thumb, an action that shames you almost as much as the half-eaten frozen nuggets.

Things People Have Asked You to Search for in Garbage Cans

Wallets
Leather gloves
Wedding rings
Keys
Paycheques
Report cards
A cherished photo of a dead grandson
X-rays
Divorce papers
A pregnancy test
A teddy bear
Their neighbour's dentures

Daylight Savings Diptych

Spring Forward

Means people will scream at you
Because it's later than they think
And now they can't get breakfast.

Fall Back

Means people will scream at you
Because it's earlier than they think
And now they can't get lunch.

Pickle Sundae

How can you refuse to make a sundae topped off with pickles when a customer explains this is how she'll tell her husband about her pregnancy? When she walks back to their table with a hot fudge sundae for him and a pickle sundae for her, he doesn't even notice at first, just stuffs his face with spoonful after spoonful until he sees the pickles in her ice cream, then hugs her so tightly you worry about the baby.

Too Much Time with the Kids

When the overwhelmed woman
with screaming kids orders
an orange pop
and a brown pop,
you ask her if she'd like
regular brown, diet brown,
or root.

Little White Spoons

Rumour had it too many customers used
the little white spoons to snort cocaine
so head office discontinued them
in favour of wooden stir sticks.

Nobody could confirm this for sure
but on the day the ever-smiling Mayor
visits the drive-thru asking
Whatever happened to those little white spoons?
you realize the rumours are true.

Cleanliness

Doug

At first you thought Doug was always prepared whenever you picked him up at 4:50 a.m., as he'd always be at his front door within seconds, but then he admitted that he slept on the couch while wearing his uniform and needed only to slip on his shoes as soon he heard your car. Ever since that day, you've never eaten the food while Doug was working the grill, for no matter how kind or rosy-cheeked you find him, his wrinkled uniform raises a cautionary flag you just can't ignore.

The Ball Room

As a child you loved the playrooms filled with thousands of colourful plastic balls, but as an adult you've seen the monstrosities children will leave behind. Each Friday evening someone needs to stay late to hose the ballroom down and remove the remnants of the prior week. During your time at the restaurant you've found numerous diapers, T-shirts bloodied from what you hope were nosebleeds, and a cornucopia of meals way past their expiry date. But of all the buried treasures, the one that sticks out most in your mind is the baby you found hidden beneath those balls, the small arm you reached down to in fear, only to realize she was someone's doll.

Napkins

Your favourite co-worker gets fired for wasting napkins, although he wasn't really wasting them, just making snowflakes for a holiday display. Everyone agrees that it's pretty stupid, so in memory of your time working together, you nickname the manager that fired him the Grinch, and hum Christmas carols whenever he walks by.

White Walls

when the white walls
start to yellow
you wipe them down
with fresh bar towels

when the white walls
start to yellow
you wipe them down
with fresh bar towels

when the white walls
start to yellow
you wipe them down
with fresh bar towels

when the white walls
start to yellow
you wipe them down
with fresh bar towels

when the white walls
start to yellow
you wipe them down
with fresh bar towels

when the white walls
start to yellow
you wipe them down
with fresh bar towels

when the white walls
start to yellow
you wipe them down
with fresh bar towels

when the white walls
start to yellow
you wipe them down
with fresh bar towels

Strawberry Sundaes

Unlike the simple push pumps for hot fudge and caramel, the ladles for strawberry never seem the right size, and no matter how many times you try to avoid it, your fingers end up red and sticky. Sometimes, no matter how often you've washed your hands, you'll find your fingers pressed below your nostrils, that sweet familiar smell relaxing you in all the commotion, an aromatherapy, a quick fix, a few seconds to yourself.

The Sky Is Falling

Like Henny Penny before her, you can't blame the customer for screaming *The sky is falling* when a pickle slice, once stuck to the ceiling, loosens and falls on her head. It's not the first time, nor will it be the last, you've seen pickle casualties, though most walk around unaware that dried up pickle has fallen onto their jackets. Once you saw one fall into a baby buggy just far enough out of reach that the baby's fingers could only dream about the strange object sent from above. You apologized to the customer and offered her a free dessert; it took all your willpower not to nudge that baby's pickle closer.

Madonna

The only thing harder
than being named Madonna
is being named Madonna
and having to wear a name tag.

Spud

One night at a party someone says
you smell like French fries
and much to your horror, it's true,
you do, you're a giant walking
French fry, a greasy potato,
someone who'll get nicknamed Spud.

Gloria

For weeks fellow workers find
G L O R I A
spelled out in French fries,
underlined in ketchup
on bare tabletops.
In the staff room a group wonders
who would do such a thing—
a teenaged girl dressed in black,
still uncertain about the meaning of life,
convinced only that her name
holds some significance;
a fan obsessed with the hit song;
or a troubled boy haunted
by the loss of his girlfriend.
At the monthly staff meeting
your manager asks to be summoned
as soon as someone finds the culprit,
but on the afternoon you spot her,

an elderly woman with shaky hands
spelling out G L O R I A,
you just sit down with her,
listen as she tells you why.

Your Favourite Washroom Graffiti

Flush twice:
it's a long way to the kitchen.

Save Room for Dessert

Days after the launch of the new
Save Room for Dessert campaign,
some joker decides to spray paint
the rooftop billboard:

> Save Room for Dessert—
> *and the rainforest.*

Usually you would find this funny,
but today your manager makes you climb up
onto a ladder with turpentine soaked rags
to remove the damage.

With every scrubbing motion
you wonder who he suspects
as the culprit behind the graffiti,
and whether you have it in you
to climb back up tonight
and paint your words again.

Thursdays

As you watch the old man with the tweezers
pluck sesame seeds off his bun

you think back to the girl from summer camp
who thought she could rub away her freckles.

Every Thursday he sits in the lobby
removing his sesame seeds

and every Thursday you think of her red hair,
the small circles she rubbed with her thumb.

The Chicken Truck

In retrospect you should have known that the snowflakes you saw weren't really snowflakes on a hot summer's day, but little white feathers from the chicken truck that overturned in front of the restaurant. All day long people found zonked out chickens hidden in the landscaping, and, unfortunately, a few were run over by customers in the drive-thru. One man screamed that he didn't take his family out for dinner to kill something. That made you think for a long time.

Value

Extra Everything

It's always middle-aged men who order everything extra: extra ketchup, extra lettuce, extra mustard. Even extra pickle. They say it in extra-loud voices and look around so they can see everyone's paying attention. The best way to deal with these customers is to make an extra effort, keep quiet, keep smiling. Tell yourself extra everything's fine.

Birds

Though management posts signs warning customers
    to beware of the birds,
each summer people get dive-bombed and lose their
    meals.

If it's a grown-up, nobody seems to care, but when
    little children get upset,
parents will scream at you to do something about it:

*It's like a horror movie out there, how can you
    expect people to eat
like that, you need to get a BB gun or some poison
    or some eagles.*

Once when a woman claimed that a bird had stolen
    a chicken nugget
right from her hand just as she was about to pop it
    into her mouth,

she said, *I just don't understand why a bird would*
   eat another bird like that;
I'm so glad humans have evolved enough to stop
   eating humans.

The Wedding

Apart from the day the funeral procession accidentally drove though the drive-thru, hearse and all, your strangest shift has to be the impromptu wedding in the parking lot. After exchanging vows, the wedding party and all their guests filed into the lobby, and while the bride struggled with her big puffy dress you overheard a bridesmaid tell her to avoid anything with mustard. This struck you as sage advice, and although you're sure it's unlikely you'll ever have to serve someone in her wedding dress again, you've made a mental note to pass it along if needed.

Coins

When some mom gets the smart idea to forego putting coins in the birthday cake and stuffs them inside the party's cheeseburgers instead, you hint that maybe this isn't such a good idea, but she's adamant and just stands there chuckling to herself as little kid after little kid stops chewing and pulls coins out of their mouths. *Isn't it wonderful*, she exclaims. *Think of all the things you can buy. You're all so very, very rich.*

Drive-Thru

Same guy at 7 a.m. for breakfast,
a little before noon for lunch,
once again while you work overtime
and he orders dinner.
Some days he drives through
a fourth time for dessert,
pretends he doesn't know you,
you don't know him.

Fish-Filletmobile

Every Friday, after a day at the fields,
the van everyone calls the fish-filletmobile
drives through with crop pickers
hungry and unable to eat the burgers.
In a heavy accent someone orders
fourteen fish burgers, parks the van for a while
then drives through again,
orders fourteen more.

Mascot

When a little old man comes up to your register, you at first think it's a practical joke, someone dressed up like the guy who steals people's hamburgers in TV commercials, and you can't help but chuckle at his humongous nose and bony body topped off with a sombrero-like black hat—especially when he orders a hamburger—but then it dawns on you how crappy it would be to look like a mascot, how on even your worst days in your polyester uniform you at least get paid.

Bulimia

You want to tell her you can see everything when she parks in the vacant lot across from the restaurant, how you swear the birds recognize her and wait until she sticks her head outside the door, finishes her business, then drives away. There's always a commotion when she leaves, a flock of seagulls, a murder of crows, any number of bird groupings you don't know the names for.

Dip Diptych

Sweet and Sour

BBQ

The Last Straw

Some little kid sticks a straw so far up his nose that he can't pull it out, and his mom screams that she's going to sue the entire goddamn chain for not having safe enough straws. Somehow, you control your laughter just long enough to tell her that you'd sue too if you saw your child like that, there ought to be a law.

Minimum Wage

After six months your manager offers
his congratulations, thanks you
for all your hard work
by giving you a twenty-five cent raise
that you'll lose in two weeks
when the minimum wage goes up.

Grimace

When your manager learns the hard way
that fat people who come in on their day off
wearing purple velour jogging suits
shouldn't be surprised
if little kids mistake them for mascots
and run up asking for treats,
you go out of your way
to mention her new haircut,
how it brings out her cheekbones,
her million-dollar smile.

100 Cheeseburgers

An elderly man you recognize as someone who moves slowly and pays for everything with change scrounged from his pockets surprises you when he pulls out a wad of bills and orders 100 cheeseburgers. You get him to repeat himself a couple of times, *100 cheeseburgers, 100 cheeseburgers* he says, tells you he intends to freeze them, they'll get him through the winter, no need for pesky walks on cold days, no danger of slipping and breaking a hip. *100 cheeseburgers will keep me going for a little while longer, at least, I don't need much.*

The Parking Lot

Since teenagers have once again spent the night before placing ketchup packets beneath the tires of parked cars, your Sunday morning looks like a crime scene—even with the happy group of seniors doing tai chi in the back. You sweep away the garbage, hose down the ketchups, and they keep on moving, their bodies tilting and weaving, their arms stroking as would a brush on canvas. Today you find yourself sweeping the asphalt more slowly, your movements fluid, the seniors hypnotic, your body moving against the fast food of it all, shifting.

ACKNOWLEDGEMENTS

This book could not have been completed without Elizabeth Bachinsky, Carolyn Smart, and Sheri-D Wilson. I sometimes wonder if they share an eye.

Thank you to the following:

The Canada Council for the Arts, Queen's University's English department, and Queen's University's President's Fund for supporting the writer-in-residency that allowed me the time to write many of these poems.

Kiss Machine, EVENT, and *Geist* for publishing early versions of some of these poems.

Lydia Avsec, Mette Bach, Ivan E. Coyote, Bernhard Friz, Wayne Grady, Jenny Hereward, Chris Hutchinson, Laurie Lewis, Day Milman, Teresa McWhirter, Merilyn Simonds, Michael V. Smith, Richard Van Camp, and everyone who has given their feedback on these poems.

My parents, Bill and Clare Nickerson, and my sister, Janet Nickerson, for laughing with me.

And to Brian, Robert, Shyla, Janice, and Susan at Arsenal Pulp Press for their ongoing support.

I'd also like to acknowledge the passing of my dear friend Matt Davy, who was and continues to be my Ideal Reader. I miss you, Bud.

OUTSTANDING EMPLOYEE

BILL N.
July, 1989

BILLEH NICKERSON is also the author of *The Asthmatic Glassblower*, nominated for the Publishing Triangle Poetry Prize, the humorous essay collection *Let Me Kiss it Better: Elixirs for the Not So Straight and Narrow*, and co-editor of *Seminal: The Anthology of Canada's Gay Male Poets* with John Barton. A founding member of the performance troupe "Haiku Night in Canada," he is the past editor of the literary journals *Event* and *Prism international*. He divides his year between Toronto and Vancouver, where he teaches creative writing at Kwantlen Polytechnic University.